Chicago Cubs
Trivia Teasers

Steve Johnson

TRAILS BOOKS
Madison, Wisconsin

Library of Congress Control Number: 2006906033
ISBN 13: 978-1931599-75-7
ISBN 10: 1-931599-75-0

Editor: Mark Knickelbine
Designer: Brian Schalk (Willems Marketing)
Photos: National Baseball Hall of Fame Library,
Cooperstown, NY

Printed in the United States of America.
11 10 09 08 07 06   6 5 4 3 2 1

Trails Books, a division of Big Earth Publishing
923 Williamson Street • Madison, WI 53703
(800) 258-5830 • www.trailsbooks.com

Contents

Albert Spalding

CHAPTER ONE

A New League—A New Team

The history of the Chicago Cubs goes way, way back. In 1870, city leaders worked to organize a strong baseball team to boost the city's image, and a team dubbed the White Stockings were born. In September of that year, the Cincinnati Red Stockings, the world's first professional baseball club, visited Chicago during part of their tour of the country. Despite Cincinnati's impressive 113-2-1 record, the White Stockings scored a huge upset with a 10-6 win. The Red Stockings returned to Chicago in October for another attempt, were thumped again by the White Stockings, 16-13, and the entire city celebrated.

When the National Association of Professional Baseball Players was formed in 1871, the White Stockings joined the league and played well until 1874, when most of their top players moved to other teams. The White Stockings lost a little snap until June of 1875, when ace pitcher Albert Spalding was signed from Boston. Spalding donned a Chicago uniform the following year and brought in several more fine players, like Ross Barnes, Cal McVey, Cap Anson, and Ezra Sutton. Meanwhile, the National Association folded due to its own difficulties, and in February of 1876 representatives from eight cities got together for a meeting in New York City to form the National League.

Along with Chicago, the new eight-team league included Boston, Louisville, New York, Philadelphia, Hartford, Cincinnati, and St. Louis. This was the official establishment of the team that would become known as the Chicago Cubs. The league has endured for over a century—2005 marked its 130th season—and the Cubs are the only remaining team of the original eight still operating in the same city.

The Cubs won the championship in the first year of the National League's existence, with strong performances by the likes of Ross Barnes, who won the batting title with a .403 average, and Spalding, who over seven years pitched in an amazing 396 Major League games, compiling a 252-68 record. Spalding's name remains on the National League's official baseball to this day, and he and others of those earliest years began a long baseball tradition in the Windy City.

Q. How were pitchers restricted in their deliveries during the 1870s?

A. It was illegal for pitchers to throw above their waists (it was not until the mid-1880s that overhand delivery was legalized).

Q. The Cubs had three different home fields in the 1870s and 1880s. Name the ballparks.

A. Twenty-third Street Grounds (1876–1877), Lakefront Park (1878–1884), and West Side Grounds (1885–1890).

Q. How was the ball-strike ratio different in the 1800s than today's standard?

A. It took nine balls for a walk, until the four-ball, three-strike count was established in 1889.

Q. One of the best player signings in baseball history occurred at the start of the 1876 season, when this star player arrived from the Philadelphia Athletics. His statistics with the Cubs are stellar: First all-time career batting average (.339, a franchise record that still stands), runs scored (1,711), hits (3,081), singles (2,330), doubles (530), RBIs (1,879), and second all-time in games played (2,253), at-bats (9,084), and triples (129). Who was this player?

A. Cap Anson.

Q. In May of 1884, this Cubs slugger became the first player in Major League history to hit three home runs in a single game. Who was he?

A. Ned Williamson.

Q. In addition to being manager of the team in 1876 and 1877, and one of the top pitchers in baseball, Albert Spalding scored big in a related business venture. What was it?

A. Sporting goods stores.

Q. Since the formation of the National League in 1876, Chicago and Boston are the only clubs, of the original eight, that have operated continuously. What other distinction does the Cubs franchise hold?

A. Chicago is the only team to have operated in one city since the birth of the National League.

Q. Many teams were shut out in early 1876 at the hands of Albert Spalding. What was the slang term associated with these regular beatings?

A. "Chicagoed." Spalding's record for the 1876 season was 47-12 with a 1.75 ERA.

Q. On September 26, 1876, the Cubs defeated which team, 7-6, to clinch the National League pennant?

A. The Hartford Dark Blues.

Q. When did the Cubs play their first regular season game at Lakefront Park?

A. May 14, 1878, in a 5-3 loss to the Indianapolis Browns.

Q. In August of 1878, after a one-year retirement, a famous Cubs player returned to play second base. Who was he?

A. Albert Spalding. It was his final regular-season game.

Q. On September 17, 1878, the Cubs and Boston tested a pitching distance of 51 feet from home plate. What was the distance used before this game?

A. 45 feet. The 60-foot, six-inch distance was eventually established in 1893.

Q. Cap Anson took charge as manager in 1879. Who did the Cubs play in the season opener?

A. The Syracuse Stars. The Cubs won, 4-3, at Lakefront Park.

Q. During an exhibition game in Indianapolis on June 26, 1879, Cap Anson was arrested. What was the charge?

A. Profanity and resisting arrest, after a squabble with a constable who was attempting to arrest Cubs players Silver Flint and Orator Schafer for unpaid bills.

Q. What was the Cubs' record in their National League pennant-winning, 1880 season?

A. 67-17.

Q. How many games did the Cubs win during their record streak in 1880?

A. 21 games. This record was outdone only one other time in Major League history, when the 1916 New York Giants won 26 in a row.

Q. George Gore set a record for stolen bases in a 12-8 win over Providence in June of 1881. How many bases did he pilfer?

A. Seven. He stole second five times and third twice.

Q. The Cubs won the pennant with a 4-0 win on September 16, 1881. Which team did they defeat?

A. Boston Red Sox.

Q. In a victory over the Worcester Ruby Legs in 1881, two consecutive Cubs batters hit home runs. Who were they?

A. King Kelly and Cap Anson.

Q. George Gore earned a nickname to accompany his reputation as one of the fastest players in the league, and in reference to his tree-trunk thighs. What was that name?

A. Piano Legs.

Q. Lakefront Park had the smallest playing field in Major League history, with a center field of just 300 feet and only 180 feet to left field. If a ball was hit over the outfield fence in 1883, what was the call?

A. A ground-rule double.

Q. What was the name of the new Cubs ballpark that opened in June of 1885?

A. West Side Grounds.

Q. Which pitcher led the league with 53 wins in 1885?

A. John Clarkson.

Q. Before Game 1 of the 1885 World Series between the Cubs and the Browns, a field event contest was held. In the throwing events, Ned Williamson won with a long-distance hurl. How far did he throw the ball?

A. 400 feet, four inches.

Q. A 21-year-old rookie struck out 13 batters for the Cubs in a win over the Kansas City Cowboys during the 1886 season. What was his name?

A. Jocko Flynn, who roared through the season with a 23-6 record.

Q. Which Cubs player led the 1886 National League in batting, runs, and on-base percentage (.388, 155, and .483, respectively)?

A. King Kelly.

Q. King Kelly was a powerhouse for the Cubs, and later with Boston, but his health declined rapidly and he died in 1894 at age 36. How did he die?

A. Pneumonia.

Q. Another Cubs great, who was also sold to Boston (early in the 1888 season), died of pneumonia at a young age (47). Who was this player?

A. John Clarkson.

Q. Which president was in office when the Cubs visited the White House in October of 1888?

A. Grover Cleveland.

Q. Name four of the five overseas nations in which the Cubs played during a world baseball tour in 1889?

A. Egypt, France, Ireland, England, and Italy.

Q. What was the reason for Ned Williamson's departure from a March 1889 game against the All-Americas, and ultimately the end of his career?

A. Ned slid into a sharp stone on the cinder-surfaced field, injuring his knee.

Q. An unusual location hosted a high-scoring (18-17) match against New York in May of 1889. The Cubs won in ten innings. Where was the game played?

A. St. George Cricket Grounds on Staten Island.

Q. The Cubs were beaten to the National League pennant in the 1890s by which three teams?

A. Boston, Baltimore, and Brooklyn.

Q. The Cubs own the all-time record for most runs in a game against Louisville in June 1897. How many runs did Chicago score?

A. 36.

Q. Which Cub's player pitched 603 innings in 71 games in 1890 and a remarkable 3,020 innings from 1889 through 1895?

A. Bill Hutchinson.

Q. Which Cubs player hit 20 career lead-off homers? (This is still the club record.)

A. Jimmy Ryan.

Q. Bill Hutchinson had some untouchable records during his career with the Cubs, including percentage of team victories. What percent of wins were credited to Hutchinson from 1890 to 1892?

A. Fifty percent or better. No pitcher since 1892 has surpassed this record.

Q. Cubs slugger Bill Dahlen rolled through the 1894 season with a record streak of hits, the longest in team history. What was his record?

A. 42 games until August 7, when Dahlen was hitless in a 13-11 win against the Reds. He also listed career records for runs, RBIs, home runs, and batting average.

Q. A devastating fire took place at which Chicago ballpark on August 5, 1894, during a game against the Cincinnati Reds?

A. West Side Grounds. More than 500 injuries were sustained by fans in a panic to escape the burning stadium. In spite of the damage to the park, a game was played there the next day, and West Side Grounds was rebuilt before the next season.

Q. On August 29, 1892, Pop Shriver and a posse of Cubs players staged a dramatic baseball event at a well-known national landmark. Where did this take place, and what was the feat?

A. Shriver caught a ball dropped from the top of the Washington Monument on the first try. Police thwarted any further attempts, as it was illegal to drop objects from the monument.

Q. Who holds the all-time high batting average for the Cubs?

A. Outfielder Bill Lange, who hit at a .389 clip during the 1895 season.

Q. Another standout in 1895 was Bill Everett, a rookie at third base. How many runs did he score that season?

A. 129.

Q. Which unlikely player stepped in at catcher in an April 1896 game against Louisville?

A. Manager Cap Anson, who was then 44 years old.

Q. What was Anson's last season as Cubs manager?

A. 1897.

Q. The Cubs earned a new nickname after the departure of Cap Anson. What was it?

A. Orphans. Anson was such a pillar of the team that his departure led the media to bestow the nickname. The Cubs merely drifted through the next several seasons without Anson's steady hand.

Gabby Hartnett

CHAPTER TWO

A New Century, and a Long Stretch of Highs and Lows

The first half of the 1900s saw many changes for Chicago's Cubs. It was a time to revel in the exciting plays of the team's superstars and cringe at the numerous "just about made it" seasons, when the team got to the championship game but couldn't quite take home the prize. Wrigley Field was built, and fans poured in to see Tinker to Evers to Chance, Gabby Hartnett's consistent greatness, and Hack Wilson blast home runs out of the park. World War II spoiled the mood, but Phil Cavaretta kept the party going. The title might not have made it to Chicago, but the support always remained, and the players responded with stubborn persistence.

Tinker, Evers, and Chance

Q. The World Series was hosted at West Side Grounds four times in the 1900s. Name the years.

A. 1906, 1907, 1908, and 1910.

Q. What nickname was bestowed on the Cubs in 1901, after the loss of many players to the American League?

A. The Remnants.

Q. The "Cubs" team name was not officially realized until the 1907 World Series. How was the name "discovered," and what were some of the 15 other nicknames for the team?

A. A sports column in the March 27, 1902, edition of the *Chicago Daily News* referred to the young rookies on the roster as "the new Cubs." The nickname caught on, and team manager Frank Chance insisted in 1907 that the name be used permanently. Some of the other nicknames used were White Stockings, Silk Stockings, Colts, Orphans, Rough Riders, Nationals, and Spuds.

Q. Which famous Cub's player made his Major League debut in September 1902, in a double-header against the Phillies?

A. Johnny Evers. Initially snubbed by teammates for being too small (5'9" and 105 pounds) for the big leagues, Evers became a solid fixture on the club until 1913, playing in 1,409 games, scoring 742 runs, and recording 1,340 hits.

Q. Joe Tinker (shortstop), Johnny Evers (second base), and Frank Chance (first base), teamed up as a famous combination for big plays. What was the play, and what popular maxim was associated with the trio?

A. The three combined talents to frustrate many an opponent with double plays. The "jingle" was "Tinker to Evers to Chance."

Q. Which team were the Cubs playing when Tinker, Evers, and Chance staged their first double play?

A. The Cincinnati Reds (Cubs lost, 8-6).

Q. The Cubs' leading hitter in 1902 was nick-named the "Human Mosquito," due to his small stature and speedy ways. Who was he?

A. Jimmy Slagle. His .315 average and 64 runs scored led the team in 1902.

Q. Jack Doscher debuted as a pitcher for the Cubs in July 1903. What distinction does he hold with his father, Herm, also a Major League player from 1879 through 1902?

A. Herm and Jack were the first father–son duo to play in the majors.

Q. Mordecai "Three-Finger" Brown was delivered to the Cubs through a trade in December 1903, and was wildly successful as a pitcher, with a 188-85 record, 346 games pitched, 1,043 strikeouts, and 49 shutouts. How did Mr. Brown receive his nickname?

A. He stuck his right hand in a corn chopper at his uncle's farm, cutting off half of his right index finger.

Q. What was the Chicago City Series?

A. A "championship" series between the Cubs and the White Sox, played just after the close of the regular season and around the same time as the World Series. The two teams met 26 times between 1903 and 1942. The Sox won a lopsided 19 times to the Cubs' 6.

Q. The Cubs played superb ball in 1904, winning 93 games, but still fell short of the pennant. Which team posted the most wins?

A. The Giants, with 106 wins.

Q. Who was the top hitter in the 1904 season, batting .310?

A. Frank Chance.

Q. Who did the Cubs play in the 1906 World Series?

A. Their cross-town rivals, the White Sox.

Q. In 1906, the Cubs set a Major League record for regular-season games won but were outdone by the White Sox (8 games to 3) in the World Series. How many games did the Cubs win?

A. 116.

Q. What position did Harry Steinfeldt play in the early 1900s?

A. Third base. He was the fourth member of the famous Tinker-Evers-Chance infield, and although Steinfeldt only played five seasons with the Cubs, four of those times the club made it to the World Series.

Q. Frank Schulte was a force for the Cubs from 1904 to 1916. What was his nickname?

A. Wildfire. Frank was very fond of actress Lillian Russell, who was in a play entitled *Wildfire*, and soon Schulte acquired that name, as well.

Q. What was special about the 1906 World Series, with the Cubs taking on the White Sox?

A. It was the first all-Chicago Series and the first time two teams from the same city played in the championship.

Q. At a July 8, 1907, game against the Dodgers in Brooklyn, Frank Chance was the focus of an angry mob of fans. What did Chance do to provoke the hostility?

A. Chance argued with the umpires for most of the game; the huge crowd would have none of it and started pitching pop bottles at him. Chance threw a few back, and pretty soon some fans were on the field to inflict more serious damage. Chance had to be escorted off the field by police and left the stadium in an armored car.

Q. What was Solly Hoffman's nickname?

A. Circus Solly, earned for his penchant for exciting circus catches.

Q. The Cubs reached the 1907 World Series against the Detroit Tigers, and some diehard fans unable to be at the games utilized a unique resource for news of the action. What was it?

A. A local pigeon aficionado brought 40 carrier pigeons to West Side Grounds; they were released at the end of each inning, delivering the latest game highlights to rabid fans.

Q. What was the score of the final game of the 1907 World Series, earning the Cubs their first world title?

A. 2-0.

Q. Who was Chicago's top hitter in the 1908 season, recording a .300 average and scoring 83 runs?

A. Johnny Evers.

Q. Which Cubs pitcher is the only player in Major League history to pitch two shutouts in one day?

A. Ed Reulbach, who blanked the Dodgers, 5-0 and 3-0, in a doubleheader on September 26, 1908.

Q. Which two players on the 1908 team hit .300 or higher?

A. Johnny Evers and Doc Marshall.

Q. Who was the starting catcher in 1908?

A. Johnny Kling.

Q. How many games did the Cubs win in 1908?

A. 99.

Q. This Cubs pitcher holds the longest consecutive win streak (14) in the Major Leagues (tied by Rick Sutcliffe in 1984).

A. Ed Reulbach, who earned the record in an 8-1 victory against the Dodgers in August 1909.

Q. What is Wrigley Field's former name?

A. Weeghman Park.

Q. In what year did the Cubs move into Weeghman Park?

A. 1916.

Q. The Cubs share a record with which team for the only dual no-hitter in pro baseball history?

A. The Cincinnati Reds, in a game on May 2, 1917. Fred Toney of the Reds and Hippo Vaughn of the Cubs threw no-hit balls in the 10th inning before Vaughn gave up a hit and lost the game.

Q. Johnny Kling and Cubs great Cap Anson faced off in a different sort of competition in Chicago in April of 1910. What was it?

A. A game of pool. Kling was an ace with the stick and won the world championship in pocket billiards in 1909.

Q. Another famous ballpark opened in Chicago in 1910. Name it.

A. Comiskey Park.

Q. The celebrated "Tinker to Evers to Chance" mantra originated with a double play in a 4-2 win over the Giants in July 1910. Franklin Adams penned a popular poem from the play. What is the poem's name?

A. "Baseball's Sad Lexicon."

Q. This Cubs pitcher led the National League in 1910 with an .833 winning percentage and a 20-4 record. Who was he?

A. King Cole.

Q. What major equipment change was established in the majors in 1910?

A. A baseball with a cork center.

Q. In addition to a two-hit, 1-0 win over the Pirates in October 1910, which Cubs pitcher boasts stats that include a 25-13 record, 1.88 ERA, 27 complete games, seven shutouts, and seven saves?

A. Three-Finger Brown.

Q. What is the Cubs' record for triples, set in 1911?

A. 101.

Q. Which Chicago slugger was the first in Major League history to belt 20 doubles, 20 triples, and 20 home runs in a single season?

A. Frank Schulte.

Q. In what year did the famous Tinker-Evers-Chance trio play their last game together?

A. 1912, in an April game against the Reds in Cincinnati. Frank Chance announced his retirement after the game.

Q. A Chicago restaurant offered a unique incentive to Frank Schulte in 1912. What was it?

A. The restaurant nailed a dinner plate to the fence in center field at West Side Grounds and declared that if Schulte broke the plate with a hit, he would collect a $10,000 prize.

Q. The volatile temper of Johnny Evers earned him a five-day suspension for an incident in a September 8, 1912, game against the Reds. What happened?

A. Evers threw dirt at umpire Brick Owens.

Q. How many home runs did pitcher Larry Cheney hit in his career?

A. One, in a 3-2 win over the Braves in Boston in 1912. In a nine-season career, Cheney had 617 at-bats.

Q. In a September 1912 game against the Dodgers, a plainclothes detective was forced to break up a fight between two Cubs players on the bench. Who were the pugilistic teammates?

A. Joe Tinker and Johnny Evers, who had a decades-long feud, allegedly over a disputed cab fare.

Q. Cubs manager Frank Chance was fired by team president Charles Murphy on September 28, 1912. Why did Murphy cut Chance?

A. Murphy stated the club lost out on the pennant because there were too many drunkards and hooligans on the team, and blamed lack of order on Chance. Chance went on to manage the Yankees and Reds, and died at age 46 in September of 1924.

Q. What was catcher George Yantz's batting average when he retired?

A. 1.000. Yantz had one career at-bat in one career game, in which he hit a single.

Q. In October of 1912, a crowd of over 30,000 at West Side Grounds became unruly, and the police had difficulty holding them back. Who assisted the police and eventually restored order?

A. The Cubs players marched with bats toward the crowd and herded the boisterous fans far back in the outfield.

Q. Johnny Evers was hired as manager for the 1913 season. How many years did Evers manage the team?

A. One season, but he came back to manage the Cubs in 1921—again for just one year.

Q. On April 12, 1913, Cubs manager Johnny Evers met an opponent who was a former teammate. Who was he?

A. Joe Tinker, manager of the Reds at the time.

Q. Which temperamental Cubs player was ejected three times in five days in June 1913?

A. Heinie Zimmerman, who tended to argue quite a bit with the umpires.

Q. Cy Williams belted in six runs and hit a grand slam in a 13-2 thumping of the Dodgers in August 1913. Which college did Williams attend as a football player, and who was his famous gridiron teammate?

A. Williams played at Notre Dame, with Knute Rockne.

Q. How many times was Johnny Evers ejected from games in 1913?

A. Best estimates say he was booted from at least 20 games.

Q. In what year was ground broken for Weeghman Park (present-day Wrigley Field) in Chicago?

A. 1914. The park was completed in seven weeks.

Q. Pitcher Jimmy Lavender caused a stir with a trick pitch in a September 1914 game against the Phillies. What did he do to raise the ire of the opposition?

A. Lavender had rubbed the ball against a piece of emery board attached to his pant leg. The game was suspended until Lavender removed the board from his pants.

Q. What was the Cubs' record in 1915, in the franchise's first losing season in 13 years?

A. 73-80.

Q. A surly fan threw an object at right fielder Wilbur Good in a June 1915 game against Cincinnati. What was the object?

A. A bullet.

Q. Jimmy Lavender injured himself in April of 1915, putting a damper on a potentially great season. How was he hurt?

A. Lavender fell while climbing out of a bathtub.

Q. When was the last regular-season game played at West Side Grounds?

A. October 3, 1915. The park was used by amateur clubs until it was torn down in 1920.

Q. What is currently on the site of the old West Side Grounds?

A. The University of Illinois Medical Center.

Q. William Wrigley, Jr. became a Cubs stockholder in 1916. How did Wrigley come by his fortune?

A. He gave away sticks of gum as incentive for customers to buy his family's soap products, and the gum earned such rave reviews that he started a chewing gum company.

Q. When did the Cubs play their first game at Weeghman Park (today's Wrigley Field)?

A. April 20, 1916. The Cubs beat the Reds, 7-6.

Q. Weeghman Park was popular with home run hitters. How many homers were belted in 1916?

A. 56, more than any other major league ballpark.

Q. What ability did catcher Jimmy Archer possess that made him stand out among his peers?

A. Archer could hurl the ball from home plate to second base from his squat position—a mighty toss.

Q. What courtesy did Charles Weeghman extend to the fans in July 1916?

A. The Cubs were the first Major League team to allow fans to keep balls hit into the stands. Prior to this, if a fan did not return a ball, he or she would be arrested for theft.

Q. Former Cub Heinie Zimmerman was suspended for life from baseball in 1919. Why?

A. He tried to convince the Giants, his team at the time, to throw a game.

Q. Fred Mitchell was hired as Chicago's manager in December 1916. He was the sixth manager in as many years. Who were the other five?

A. Frank Chance, Johnny Evers, Hank O'Day, Roger Bresnahan, and Joe Tinker.

Q. Which three future NFL Hall of Fame stars played in a Cubs–Reds game in July 1917?

A. Paddy Driscoll, Greasy Neale, and Jim Thorpe.

Q. The gate receipts from a June 1917 Cubs-Cardinals game were donated to which charitable organization?

A. The Red Cross.

Q. Al Demaree was a star for the Cubs, but his post-career ambitions were his bigger hit. What was Demaree's claim to fame?

A. He was a celebrated sports cartoonist. His cartoons appeared in more than 200 newspapers and were a fixture in *The Sporting News* for more than 30 years.

Q. The Cubs made a blunder of a trade in 1918, sending Cy Williams to the Phillies. How many home runs did Williams end his career with?

A. 251. Only Babe Ruth and Rogers Hornsby hit more career homers.

Q. Only one Cubs player was sent to military service during World War I. Who was he?

A. Grover Alexander.

Q. Why did the National Commission end the 1918 season on September 2?

A. The draft rules required qualifying men to enter the military or work in a war-related job.

Q. Which team did the Cubs play in the 1918 World Series?

A. The Boston Red Sox, with Babe Ruth pitching two of the games.

Q. What military event took place before Game 1 of the 1918 Series?

A. Sixty Army planes flew over Comiskey Park, the first flyover at a sporting event.

Q. What was Weeghman Park called after Weeghman resigned in 1918?

A. Cubs Park. The new name took effect in the 1919 season.

Q. How long was the shortest nine-inning game in Cubs history?

A. 58 minutes, in which the Cubs beat the Braves 3-0 in a September 1919 contest.

Q. The Cubs were hugely popular with fans. How many supporters cheered on the team in 1927?

A. Chicago was the first National League team to attract over one million fans in a season.

Q. The Cubs won, 26-23, over which team, in the highest scoring game in Major League history?

A. The Phillies.

Q. The Cubs played the Cardinals at Sportsman's Park in St. Louis in 1920. What was that park renamed in 1953?

A. Busch Stadium.

Q. Grover Alexander helped the Cubs win a 1-0 match against the Dodgers on August 28, 1920. What was the landmark rights event that took place only two days earlier?

A. The 19th Amendment was passed, and women were granted the right to vote.

Q. Which Cubs star player replaced Fred Mitchell as manager in October 1920?

A. Johnny Evers.

Q. Charlie Hollocher boasted a huge year in 1922, with a .340 average and over 200 hits, but he also set a dubious team record in the same season. What was it?

A. He was caught stealing bases 29 times.

Q. Left fielder Lawrence "Hack" Miller came to the Cubs with some unique abilities. Name them.

A. He was a circus strongman and winner of several weightlifting championships. He also drove nails through boards with his fists, and bent iron bars, and uprooted trees.

Q. How big was Cubs pitcher Ernest "Tiny" Osborne?

A. The 6' 4", 215-pound Osborne pitched for the Cubs from 1922 through 1924.

Q. Grover Alexander set a Cubs record for innings pitched without walks in the 1923 season. What is the record?

A. Alexander pitched 51 consecutive innings without recording a walk.

Q. Which positions did Jigger Statz play in his six-year tenure with the Cubs?

A. Second base, third base, and shortstop.

Q. Three Cubs pitchers won 15 games or more in 1924. Who were they?

A. Vic Aldridge, Vic Keen, and Tony Kaufmann.

Q. Grover Alexander won his 300th game on September 20, 1924, against which team?

A. The New York Giants.

Q. Which Cubs player's ashes were scattered at Wrigley Field after his death in 1983?

A. Charlie Grimm.

Q. In 1925, the Cubs celebrated their 50th season in the National League, but their record wasn't so jolly. What was it?

A. 68-86.

Q. What was the name of the celebration hosted by the National League, recognizing its 50th year?

A. The Golden Jubilee.

Q. Only one other team joined the Cubs as members of the National League for all fifty seasons. Name the team.

A. The Braves.

Q. Who is known as the greatest catcher in Cubs history?

A. Gabby Hartnett, who played with the club from 1922 to 1940.

Q. Guy Bush won only six games as a rookie in 1925, but finished his career with how many victories?

A. 176.

Q. Umpire Frank Wilson ejected eleven Cubs in an August 1925 doubleheader with the Dodgers. Why did he jettison so many players?

A. They all questioned his calls on the field.

Q. There was a ballpark named Wrigley Field in another city. Name the city.

A. Los Angeles.

Q. Why wasn't new manager Joe McCarthy initially accepted at his post?

A. He had never managed, or even played, in the Major Leagues before arriving in Chicago.

Q. How many home runs did Hack Wilson hit in his first season with the Cubs?

A. A league-leading 21.

Q. Charlie Root was an ace pitcher in 1926. How many games did he win that season, and what was his total number of wins with the Cubs?

A. 18 in 1926 and a total of 201.

Q. Which player was the first to hit a homer off of the scoreboard at Cubs Park?

A. Hack Wilson, in a game against the Braves in May 1926.

Q. What was the "secret dark liniment" Cubs trainers used to keep Guy Bush's arm loose?

A. Coca-Cola.

Q. In November of 1926, Cubs Park was christened with a new name. What was it?

A. Wrigley Field.

Q. How many innings made up the longest game in Cubs history?

A. 22 innings, against the Braves in May 1927.

Q. Which Cubs player completed an unassisted triple play in a 7-6 win over the Pirates in 1927? Name the player and his position.

A. Jimmy Cooney, shortstop. This triple play is the only one in Cubs history; only twelve have been made in Major League history.

Q. How was Giants manager John McGraw injured after a game at Wrigley Field in May 1928?

A. He was hit by a car while crossing the street, breaking his leg.

Q. Riggs Stephenson had a .324 batting average in 1928. What is his career average with the Cubs?

A. Stephenson played from 1926 through 1934 with a career average of .336.

Q. In November 1928, Chicago acquired a player from the Braves who, in the following year, had one of the strongest seasons in Cubs history, posting a .380 batting average, 156 runs, 39 home runs, and 229 hits. Who was the player?

A. Rogers Hornsby.

Q. In 1929, the Cubs signed the youngest player ever contracted by a Major League team. Who was the player, and how old was he?

A. Red Solomon, 13 years old.

Q. How did Norm McMillan score his "invisible" grand slam in a game against the Reds at Wrigley Field in August of 1929?

A. McMillan's hit sailed down the left field line and appeared to vanish in an open gutter. The Reds' Evar Swanson thought the ball might have rolled into Cubs pitcher Ken Penner's jacket in the bullpen. Swanson failed to find the ball, and during the search all of the base runners had scored for the Cubs. Later, Penner found the ball lodged in the sleeve of his jacket.

Q. What was the attendance record for the Cubs in 1929?

A. 1,485,166 loyal fans.

Q. What is the Cubs' record for grand slams in a season?

A. Nine, recorded in 1929.

Q. What was the Cubs' National League-leading record in the 1930s?

A. 889-648, and a winning percentage of .579. The team danced through the decade without a single losing season.

Q. How many winning decades have the Cubs had since the 1930s?

A. Zero.

Q. In what year did William Wrigley, Jr. pass away, and who took over ownership of the team?

A. Wrigley passed away in 1932, and his son, Philip, became the new owner.

Q. How many home runs did Hack Wilson blast in 1930?

A. 56, along with 191 RBIs.

Q. Cubs pitcher Hal Carlson died suddenly at the age of 36, on May 28, 1930. How did he die?

A. Hemorrhage of the stomach. Carlson had long endured ulcers and even predicted he might die from the malady.

Q. Kiki Cuyler had a .355 batting average in 1930. He also led the league in stolen bases and the Cubs in doubles. How many of each did he have?

A. 37 stolen bases and 50 doubles.

Q. Ladies' Day at Wrigley Field on June 6, 1930, attracted 30,476 female fans, who were admitted free. What was the result of this big day for the ladies?

A. A complete change in policy. Women were no longer admitted free, and female fans had to request tickets by mail to the Cubs' office.

Q. The Cubs set a National League home run record in 1930. How many did they hit?

A. 171.

Q. In what year were night games introduced in the Major Leagues?

A. 1935.

Q. When was the first night game at Wrigley Field?

A. 1988.

Q. What record did Hack Wilson break in a game against the Pirates?

A. The National League home-run record, with 44.

Q. In a September 20, 1930, game against the Braves, Hack Wilson broke the Major League RBI record of 175. Wilson's 176 bested whose record?

A. Lou Gehrig.

Q. Wilson hit two home runs against the Reds on September 27, 1930. What was Wilson's homer total with that pair?

A. 56.

Q. Wilson's 56 home runs in 1930 was solid as the National League record until which two players went far beyond that number?

A. Mark McGwire with 70 and Sammy Sosa with 66, both in the home-run derby of 1998.

Q. What is the Cubs' team record for doubles during a season?

A. 340, in 1931.

Q. At a doubleheader in St. Louis in July of 1931, nearly 46,000 fans overflowed Sportsman's Park, and many watched the game from the outfield. What was the outcome of a ball hit into the crowd?

A. The opposing team had such difficulty fielding, or even finding, balls hit into the boisterous fans that those hits were automatically ruled ground-rule doubles.

Q. Why did catcher Jimmy Archer receive a medal from the National Safety Council on August 7, 1931?

A. He saved two men from a truck after they had succumbed to carbon monoxide fumes.

Q. Which Cubs 1975 Hall of Fame inductee was knocked out of the game by a pitch in his first Major League appearance?

A. Billy Herman, in a 1931 game against the Reds at Wrigley Field.

Q. Why did the sale of lemons in Chicago soar in the 1920s and 1930s?

A. Fans smuggled the fruit into games to hurl at players and umpires who displeased them. Rogers Hornsby was especially a favorite target.

Q. Which famous Cubs player was recognized in Chicago on September 20, 1931, as the Cubs crushed the Giants in both games of a doubleheader?

A. It was Gabby Hartnett Day.

Q. How old was William Wrigley, Jr. when he died on January 26, 1932?

A. William was 70 years old at his passing.

Q. What color were the new Cubs uniforms in 1932?

A. Black and gold.

Q. What other major change to the Cubs' uniforms took place in 1932?

A. The players wore numbers on their uniforms for the first time. Numbers 1 through 7 matched their batting order.

Q. How was Billy Jurges hurt in a 1932 incident with a lady friend of questionable character?

A. Violet Valli shot Jurges with a pistol. Luckily, his wounds were minor and he was back in action in less than three weeks.

Q. In the fall of 1932, the Cubs fired Rogers Hornsby as manager. Who took over the reins?

A. Charlie Grimm.

Q. Which team did the Cubs play in the 1932 World Series?

A. The Yankees.

Q. Who won the first game of that Series?

A. The Yankees, 12-6.

Q. What was all the hubbub with Babe Ruth in the fifth inning of Game 3 of the 1932 World Series?

A. With a 2-2 count and Wrigley Field fans booing him, Ruth appeared to gesture to center field, and, on the next pitch from Charlie Root, belted a home run over the fence. The homer is known as "Ruth's called shot."

Q. What happened in Los Angeles on March 10, 1933, while the Cubs were in town for spring training?

A. An earthquake shook the city, causing widespread damage and 120 deaths.

Q. Which team did the Cubs play at Wrigley Field in L.A. the day the quake hit?

A. The New York Giants; the Cubs lost, 5-3.

Q. With Prohibition coming to an end, what changed at Wrigley Field at an April 12 , 1933, game against the Cardinals?

A. Beer was sold at the ballpark for the first time since 1919.

Q. The Cubs rescheduled a game in Chicago against the Braves on May 27, 1933. What was the reason?

A. The opening day of the World's Fair, held that year in Chicago.

Q. What influence did the World's Fair have on baseball?

A. The All-Star Game was conceived (by *Chicago Tribune* sports editor Arch Ward) and became an annual affair.

Q. How many hits did Billy Jurges record at a June 28, 1933, doubleheader against the Phillies?

A. Six.

Q. What kept Jurges busy the morning of those games?

A. He got married in Reading, Pennsylvania.

Q. Which Cubs players were in the first All-Star game, on July 6, 1933?

A. Lon Warneke, Gabby Hartnett, and Woody English.

Q. In July 1933, Warneke gained the distinction of being the only pitcher to do what in the All-Star game?

A. He is the only pitcher in the history of the All-Star game to smack a triple.

Q. Gabby Hartnett hit a grand slam in a 7-1 win over the Reds in September 1933. How many homers did Gabby hit that year?

A. He concluded the season with 16 home runs.

Q. On Opening Day of the 1934 season, which Cubs pitcher clobbered the Reds with a one-hit game, 13 strikeouts, and a 6-0 victory?

A. Lon Warneke, in what is considered the best Opening Day pitching performance in Cubs history.

Q. The Cubs had their best start in club history in 1934. How many games did they win to start the season?

A. Seven.

Q. Who is the only Cub to pitch shutouts in his first two Major League starts?

A. Bill Lee, blanking the Phillies and Dodgers in May 1934.

Q. A tall Louisiana boy, what was Bill Lee's nickname?

A. "General."

Q. Pitcher Jim Weaver was the tallest player in the Major Leagues in the 1930s. How tall was he?

A. 6' 6".

Q. How many games did Bill Lee win as a Cub?

A. 139.

Q. What nighttime event was held at Wrigley Field on September 25, 1934, with the assistance of portable lighting?

A. The world heavyweight wrestling title, with Jim Londos taking on Ed "Strangler" Lewis.

Q. Which player hit a home run on his first pitch of his first Major League game in 1934?

A. Phil Cavaretta.

Q. How old was Cavaretta when he joined the Cubs?

A. Eighteen.

Q. Cavaretta played with the Cubs until 1954 and recorded impressive statistics. What were his numbers for games played, runs scored, home runs, and RBIs?

A. 1,953 games played, 968 runs scored, 92 home runs, and 896 RBIs.

Q. Which marquee player did the Cubs miss out on in late 1934, due to P.K. Wrigley's refusal to pony up the money? Hint: the player eventually wore a Yankees uniform.

A. Joe DiMaggio.

Q. Which team did the Cubs face in the 1935 World Series, and what was the outcome?

A. The Detroit Tigers. The Cubs lost, four games to two.

Q. Charlie Grimm retired as a player in 1935. Who replaced him as starting first baseman?

A. Phil Cavaretta.

Q. When did the Cubs play their first night game?

A. July 1, 1935, against the Reds at Crosley Field in Cincinnati.

Q. What was the beef between Billy Jurges and Walter Stephenson that led to fisticuffs during a July 1935 game against the Pirates in Pittsburgh?

A. Jurges teased Stephenson, a North Carolina native, about the Confederacy's loss in the Civil War.

Q. The Cubs embarked on a long winning streak in 1935, beginning with a victory over the Phillies in September. How many games did they subsequently win?

A. Twenty-one.

Q. Phil Cavaretta won a 1-0 game for the Cubs on September 25, 1935, with a home run against the Cardinals. What was special about this win?

A. He accomplished the same feat on the same day the previous year.

Q. Who is the youngest player in the history of the World Series?

A. Phil Cavaretta, at age 19.

Q. Cubs fan James Ridner wagered a unique bet that the Cubs would win the Series in 1935. What was his penance for the lost bet?

A. He pushed a baby carriage, carrying the winner of the bet, 550 miles from Kentucky to Tiger Stadium in Detroit.

Q. Billy Herman was a star for the Cubs in the 1936 season. How many doubles did he record that year?

A. 57, tying his mark from the previous year.

Q. "The Star-Spangled Banner" was played only on special occasions during the early years of baseball. When did the patriotic tune become a regular part of games?

A. In 1942, with World War II in full swing.

Q. Which five radio stations broadcasted Cubs and White Sox games in 1936?

A. WGN, WIND, WBBM, WCFL, and WJJD.

Q. During a game at Wrigley Field against the Phillies in June of 1936, trainer Andy Lotshaw went to the aid of a woman who had been knocked silly by a foul ball. Lotshaw knew the woman when he arrived. Who was she?

A. His wife.

Q. Which avenue of employment did Ethan Allen take after his career ended?

A. Writing and inventing All-Star Baseball, a tabletop game.

Q. Which college team did Ethan Allen coach?

A. Yale, with a twenty-three-year tenure.

Q. Which famous individual, coached by former Cub's player Ethan Allen, played first base for Yale in 1947 and 1948 NCAA championship games?

A. Future President George Herbert Walker Bush.

Q. Tex Carleton boasted a 7-12 record in 1936. The seven wins came with the clobbering of which team?

A. All seven of Carleton's wins were against the Braves.

Q. The Cubs were the first team in baseball to install this item in the dugout (in April 1937). What was the item?

A. A bat rack.

Q. What significant event occurred on May 6, 1937, the day on which the Cubs beat the Phillies, 1-0?

A. The Hindenburg burst into flames over New Jersey.

Q. What famous item was added to Wrigley Field in 1937?

A. The famous ivy was planted on Wrigley's outfield walls.

Q. How many consecutive batters did Clay Bryant retire in a July 14, 1938, game against the Phillies?

A. 23, from the first through eighth innings.

Q. The Cubs fired Charlie Grimm as manager in July of 1938. Who took over the role?

A. Gabby Hartnett.

Wrigley Field, circa 1950.

CHAPTER THREE

The Lovable Losers

The second half of the twentieth century was a frustrating time for the Cubs. The club continued to make valiant efforts at establishing winning ways, and fans retained hope that their championship dreams would finally be fulfilled. The 1950s were the worst ten years in Cubs history, but Ernie Banks won two MVP awards. The team struggled mightily in the 1960s but rebounded in 1967 with six consecutive winning seasons. There were flashes of hope late in many seasons, but the Cubs always seemed to unravel at pennant time. The 1980s brought two Eastern Division pennants, but those were the only two winning seasons in that ten-year stretch. The club only saw the postseason once in the 1990s (1998), but that year included Sammy Sosa's incredible 66 home runs.

Q. What position did Grimm take after getting the boot?

A. He was radio commentator for Cubs and White Sox games for stations WBBM and WJJD.

Q. In a September 1938 game against the Reds, pitcher Charlie Root faced Douglas Corrigan in the sixth inning, only to have play stopped for a publicity stunt. What was the delay?

A. After being denied clearance to fly his dilapidated plane to Ireland, Corrigan filed a bogus flight plan to California and flew instead across the ocean to Dublin. He blamed his directional troubles on a broken compass, but the maneuver earned him the nickname "Wrong Way" Corrigan, and he became an instant celebrity. The stunt at the Cubs–Reds game involved Corrigan arriving late at the park, then playfully ticking a pitch from Root into the infield and running to third base.

Q. Which player hit a grand slam to pace Chicago to a 6-3 win over the Braves on September 14, 1938, in Boston?

A. Gabby Hartnett.

Q. Hartnett smacked another homer two weeks later at a fog-shrouded game against the Pirates at Wrigley Field, to win the pennant for the Cubs. The hit is said to be the greatest moment in Cubs history. What name was the event given?

A. Homer in the Gloamin'.

Q. Who were the Cubs' opponents in the 1938 World Series?

A. The New York Yankees.

Q. What was the score, and who prevailed in Game One of the 1938 Series?

A. Yankees won, 3-1.

Q. What was outfielder Bill Nicholson's nickname?

A. "Swish," named for his commanding swings.

Q. Who was the first Cub's player to wear number 13 on his uniform?

A. Claude Passeau.

Q. Which other Cubs players wore number 13?

A. Hal Manders, Bill Faul, Turk Wendell, Jeff Fassero, Rey Ordonez, and Neifi Perez.

Q. Dizzy Dean started off the 1939 season with a three-hit shutout of which team?

A. The Boston Braves.

Q. A different color ball was used briefly in the late 1930s. What color was it?

A. Yellow.

Q. When was the last time the Cubs played in the World Series?

A. 1945, against the Detroit Tigers. The Tigers won the title.

Q. In 1940, the Cubs were the first team to experiment with a significant modification to their uniforms. What was the change?

A. They tried sleeveless uniforms, but the players balked at the new duds and they returned to the traditional game wear in 1943.

Q. Who took over at catcher for Gabby Hartnett in 1940?

A. Al Todd.

Q. The Cubs had a strong outfield in the 1940 season. Name the players.

A. Jim Gleeson, Hank Leiber, and Bill Nicholson.

Q. What were some of Stan Hack's statistics during the 1940 season? Name three for a correct answer.

A. The Cubs' third baseman had a .317 average, 101 runs, 191 hits, 38 doubles, and 21 stolen bases.

Q. The Cubs brought up Lou Novikoff from the Pacific Coast League in August of 1940. What was Lou's nickname?

A. "The Mad Russian."

Q. What "first" did the Cubs claim in 1941 with an addition to Wrigley Field?

A. They were the first team to install an organ at their stadium.

Q. The Cubs signed Dizzy Dean as a coach in 1941, but he only held that title for seven weeks. What was his next role?

A. Broadcasting, including both radio and television.

Q. When were batting helmets first used throughout the Major Leagues?

A. The 1950s.

Q. Which team did Cubs treasurer Bill Veeck, Jr. and coach Charlie Grimm purchase in June of 1941?

A. The Milwaukee Brewers.

Q. What career choice did Larry French make after playing for the Cubs in 1941 and the Dodgers in 1942?

A. He entered the Navy, retiring as a captain in the Naval Reserves in 1969.

Q. Who is the only Cubs pitcher to win 200 games?

A. Charlie Root, who chalked up number 200 in August 1941, with a 6-4 win over the Braves.

Q. P. K. Wrigley set aside material to construct and install lights at Wrigley Field after the 1941 season, but did not erect them. Why not?

A. Wrigley donated the material to the War Department after the attack on Pearl Harbor.

Q. Which Cubs players were in the military at the beginning of the 1942 season?

A. Walt Lanfranconi, Russ Meyers, and Eddie Waitkus.

Q. What happened to balls hit into the stands during the World War II years?

A. The fans returned the balls, which were then donated to the Armed Forces recreation divisions.

Q. What record did Braves pitcher Jim Tobin set in a 6-5 win over the Cubs in May of 1942?

A. Tobin is the only pitcher in the history of the Major Leagues to hit three home runs in a single game.

Q. Jimmie Foxx was 34 years old when he arrived in Chicago with a résumé that included 524 home runs (with the Philadelphia Athletics and Boston Red Sox). What is significant about his home run record?

A. No player has hit 524 homers at a younger age than 34.

Q. On Salvage Day at Wrigley Field in September of 1942, how were women admitted to the game for free?

A. Entrance was on the house if they brought two pounds of scrap metal.

Q. The gate receipts from the Cubs-Reds game in May 1942 were donated to the Army-Navy Relief Fund. Who won the game?

A. The Reds bested the Cubs 10-1.

Q. The All-American Girls Professional Baseball League was formed by P. K. Wrigley in 1943, with four teams. From where did the teams hail?

A. Rockford, Illinois; South Bend, Indiana; Racine, Wisconsin; and Kenosha, Wisconsin.

Q. What popular Hollywood movie was inspired by the women's league?

A. *A League of Their Own.*

Q. In what year did Charlie Grimm return as manager of the Cubs?

A. 1944.

Q. At a July 1944 doubleheader against the Giants at Wrigley Field, several former Cubs stars sold war bonds to fans. Who were the players?

A. Three-Finger Brown, Jimmy Archer, Rogers Hornsby, Fred Lindstrom, and Hippo Vaughn.

Q. How many hits did Phil Cavaretta have in 1944?

A. 197.

Q. Who is the only player in team history to hit home runs in four consecutive at-bats?

A. Bill Nicholson, against the New York Giants in July 1944.

Q. Prior to June 1945, the scoreboard at Wrigley Field was a reddish brown. What color was it painted in 1945?

A. Green.

Q. Who was the National League MVP in 1945?

A. Phil Cavaretta.

Q. What historic world event occurred just five days before a Cubs 20-6 win over the Dodgers on August 11, 1945?

A. The United States dropped the atom bomb on Hiroshima, Japan.

Q. What is "The Curse of the Billy Goat?"

A. After local restaurant owner Billy Sianis was denied admission to a game at Wrigley Field with his pet goat, he put a hex on the Cubs and said they would never again play in the World Series.

Q. What was the name of Sianis' Chicago restaurant?

A. The Billy Goat Tavern.

Q. What was the tavern's claim to fame in the 1970s?

A. It was a favorite haunt of members of the Second City comedy team, which included the likes of John Belushi and Dan Aykroyd.

Q. Where did the Cubs hold training camp prior to the 1946 season?

A. Catalina Island, off the coast of southern California.

Q. In April 1946, station WBKB had the distinction of broadcasting the first televised Cubs game. Who was the commentator?

A. "Whispering Joe" Wilson.

Q. Pitcher Claude Passeau was an ace fielder. How many fielding attempts did he make without an error in the 1941–1946 seasons?

A. 273, a record that still stands.

Q. Why did Passeau wear the smallest glove in the Major Leagues?

A. A childhood shotgun accident left two fingers of his left hand permanently bent.

Q. Peanuts Lowrey was a successful actor, as well as a solid performer for the Cubs. What were some of his acting credits?

A. The *Our Gang* comedies as well as movies, including *Pride of the Yankees*, *The Stratton Story*, and *The Winning Team*.

Q. In what year was the All-Star Game first played at Wrigley Field?

A. 1947.

Q. Which team emerged the victor in that game?

A. The American League, 2-1.

Q. How many players have hit the center field scoreboard at Wrigley Field?

A. None to this date.

Q. The Cubs' dismal 1948 season inspired a famous Norman Rockwell painting that appeared in *The Saturday Evening Post.* What was the painting's title?

A. "Bottom of the Ninth."

Q. What was pitcher Cal McLish's celebrity status with the Cubs?

A. He has the longest name in franchise history: Calvin Coolidge Julius Caesar Tuskahoma McLish.

Q. Who was the first African American to play for the Cubs?

A. Ernie Banks, in 1953.

Q. Who took over the role of manager for Charlie Grimm in 1949?

A. Frankie Frisch.

Q. What troubles came to Eddie Waitkus (who would be the inspiration for the movie *The Natural*) on June 14, 1949, at the Edgewater Beach Hotel in Chicago?

A. He was shot with a .22 rifle by an obsessed fan. Eddie was banged up but returned to play in 1950.

Q. Which future Hall of Fame Cubs players took part in an old-timers game at Wrigley Field in July of 1949?

A. Gabby Hartnett, Rogers Hornsby, Ray Schalk, Ted Lyons, Red Faber, and Max Carey.

Q. Roy Smalley had a less-than-stellar career with Chicago. What was the name of the performance club he was associated with?

A. The "20-50 Club"—21 home runs and 51 errors.

Q. Which Cub's star won the MVP award in 1958 and 1959?

A. Ernie Banks.

Q. What happened to Andy Lotshaw during a thunderstorm-delayed game at Wrigley Field in June 1950?

A. He was knocked to the floor of the clubhouse by a direct hit of lightning.

Q. What famous TV and movie actor played for the Cubs in 1950?

A. Chuck Connors.

Q. Who was the first native of Chicago hired to manage the Cubs?

A. Phil Cavaretta, in 1951.

Q. What was Randy Jackson's nickname, and how was it bestowed?

A. "Handsome Ransom." Ransom was Jackson's given name, and his likeness to actor Gregory Peck earned him the complimentary title.

Q. Who won the MVP award in 1952?

A. Left fielder Hank Sauer, who led the league with 37 home runs and 121 RBIs.

Q. With 17 wins to his credit, which Cubs pitcher led the team to a .500 record in 1952?

A. Bob Rush.

Q. On June 20, 1953, the Cubs lost to the Dodgers on a horribly hot day at Wrigley Field. How hot was it?

A. 104 degrees, the highest temperature in Chicago history.

Q. While Ernie Banks was the first African American to play in a game with the Cubs, who was the first on the Cubs roster?

A. Second baseman Gene Baker.

Q. Ernie Banks is known as "Mr. Cub." How many games and home runs did he pile up during his career?

A. 2,528 games and 512 homers.

Q. Phil Cavaretta was fired as manager in 1954. Who replaced him?

A. Stan Hack.

Q. The Cubs got Steve Bilko in a trade from the Cardinals in April of 1954. What television credit does Bilko hold?

A. Phil Silvers named the Sgt. Bilko character after Steve Bilko.

Q. One of the most famous names in baseball, Joe Garagiola, played for the Cubs in 1953 and 1954. What was his career after he retired in 1954?

A. He had a very successful run in broadcasting, lending his personality to the World Series, All-Star game, Game of the Week, and the *Today Show*.

Q. Why was Sam Jones called "Toothpick Sam?"

A. He pitched with a toothpick in his mouth.

Q. Ernie Banks was the first player in the history of pro baseball to hit over four grand slams in one season. How many did he hit and how long did he hold the record?

A. Five slams, and the record stood until 1987.

Q. Who broke Banks' record?

A. Don Mattingly hit six in 1987.

Q. Who were the popular radio voices for Cubs games in 1956 on station WIND?

A. Jack Quinlan, Gene Elston, and Milo Hamilton.

Q. What was added to the dugout in the 1956 season to help the players recover faster after extreme efforts on the field?

A. Oxygen.

Q. Ernie Banks missed the first game of his career in August of 1956. How many consecutive games did he play to that point?

A. 424, a record that still stands.

Q. What was the contraption called that moved fans to the upper deck at Wrigley Field in 1956?

A. The "Speed-Walk," a moving ramp that often malfunctioned and was removed in 1960.

Q. Which three Cubs pitchers worked to set an unwelcome record in 1957 by walking nine batters in one inning (in a 9-5 loss to the Reds on April 24)?

A. Moe Drabowsky, Jim Brosnan, and Jackie Collum.

Q. How many home runs did the Cubs hit in the 1958 season?

A. 182, a club record.

Q. Stan Musial of the Cardinals whacked his 3,000th hit in May of 1958 at Wrigley Field. Who was the Cubs pitcher?

A. Moe Drabowsky.

Q. Who is the youngest pitcher in Cubs history?

A. Dick Ellsworth, who was 18 when he signed with the team.

Q. Superstar Ernie Banks led the National League in home runs in the 1958 season with how many?

A. 47.

Q. Who did the Cubs play in their first-ever road game televised in Chicago?

A. The Cardinals, in August 1958.

Q. From 1959 through 1962, how many All-Star games were played each season? Hint: It's more than one.

A. Two.

Q. Dale Long hit a pinch-hit home run on two consecutive at-bats in August of 1959. What other Cubs players have accomplished the same feat?

A. Carmen Fanzone, Darrin Jackson, and Henry Rodriguez.

Q. P. K. Wrigley fired manager Bob Scheffing in 1959. Who was Scheffing's replacement?

A. Charlie Grimm, who was 61 years old at the time.

Q. In what year were Cubs games first telecast in color?

A. 1960.

Q. Ron Santo hit his first home run in 1960. How old was he at the time?

A. 20 years old.

Q. How many total homers did Santo hit while playing for the Cubs?

A. 337.

Q. Ernie Banks led the National League with how many home runs in 1960?

A. 41.

Q. Banks hit his 231st home run in April 1960, and was the all-time Cubs leader in that regard. How long did his record stand, and who broke it?

A. Sammy Sosa broke the record in 2004.

Q. Who was the youngest Cubs player to hit a home run?

A. 18-year-old Danny Murphy, in September 1960.

Q. How many home runs did outfielder Billy Williams blast in his career?

A. 426.

Q. Which Cubs sluggers are the only ones to hit more homers than Williams?

A. Sammy Sosa and Ernie Banks.

Q. Which position did Ernie Banks try in 1961, in a departure from his regular shortstop responsibility?

A. Left field.

Q. What position did Banks eventually play full time?

A. First base.

Q. Billy Williams is third all time in games played for Chicago, behind only Ernie Banks and Cap Anson. How many did Williams play?

A. 2,213.

Q. How long was Ernie Banks' streak of consecutive games played?

A. 717, from 1956 through 1961.

Q. How many teams were included in the National League after its expansion in 1962?

A. Ten.

Q. The Cubs struck out 18 times in a loss to which Dodgers pitcher in April of 1962?

A. Sandy Koufax.

Q. The Cubs brought on board the first African-American coach in Major League history in 1962. Who was he?

A. Buck O'Neill.

Q. Which Cubs player smacked a home run into the center field bleachers, more than 450 feet from home plate, at the Polo Grounds in June of 1962?

A. Lou Brock.

Q. Who won the second 1962 All-Star game at Wrigley Field?

A. The American League, 9-4.

Q. What tune did the organist play during a bitterly cold game against the Dodgers in April of 1963?

A. "Jingle Bells."

Q. Pitcher Bob Buhl holds the longest hitless streak in Major League history. What is his gloomy record?

A. 0 for 88 in 1963.

Q. What was the "Whitlow fence?"

A. Bob Whitlow, the team athletic director at the time, suggested an eight-foot wire fence on top of the centerfield wall for a better hitting background.

Q. Billy Williams racked up a huge pile of consecutive games played through 1970. How many did he play?

A. 1,117.

Q. When did the Cubs first play at Shea Stadium in New York?

A. April 1964.

Q. Which three players each drove in more than 100 runs in the 1965 season?

A. Ron Santo, Ernie Banks, and Billy Williams.

Q. Ted Abernathy holds the Cubs' single-season record for pitching appearances in a season. How many times did Ted take the mound in the 1965 season?

A. 84.

Q. Where did the Cubs play their first indoor game?

A. The Houston Astrodome, in 1965.

Q. Against which team did Ernie Banks hit his 400th career home run in 1965?

A. The Cardinals.

Q. Who was the surprise new manager of the Cubs in October of 1965?

A. Leo Durocher.

Q. In 1966, the Cubs moved their spring training camp from Mesa, Arizona, to what new location?

A. Long Beach, California.

Q. The Cubs utilized a great number of catchers from the 1940s through 1965. How many played that position?

A. Fifty different men worked behind the plate.

Q. After Ron Santo suffered a fractured cheekbone in a game against the Mets in 1966, he became the first Cub's player to use what new equipment on the field?

A. An earflap on his batting helmet.

Q. In what year did earflaps become mandatory in the Major Leagues?

A. 1971.

Q. How old was pitcher Robin Roberts when he signed with the Cubs in 1966?

A. 39.

Q. What set Leo Durocher off at the end of a game at the Astrodome in August of 1966, causing him to rip the phone out of the dugout wall?

A. The animated scoreboard was making fun of him with cartoons displayed to the fans.

Q. Which superstar celebrity joined his buddy Leo Durocher at an exhibition game in Palm Springs, California, in March of 1967?

A. Frank Sinatra.

Q. What material was installed at Wrigley Field in 1967 over the empty seats in center field, and why?

A. Green Astroturf covered the seats to improve the background for batters. The Astroturf was removed in 1982.

Q. What did Ferguson Jenkins do to stay busy during his first few off-seasons in the late 1960s?

A. He played basketball for the Harlem Globetrotters.

Q. The Cubs were in first place in July of 1967. How long had it been since they held that spot as late as July?

A. Twenty-two years, last seen in 1945.

Q. Which two brothers pitched against each other for the first time at a game in Atlanta in July of 1967?

A. Phil (Braves) and Joe (Cubs) Niekro.

Q. Who played third base for the Cubs in the 1960s and early 1970s?

A. Ron Santo.

Q. What tragic event led to the postponement of Opening Day in 1968?

A. The assassination of Dr. Martin Luther King, Jr.

Q. What change took place in the National League in 1969, due to the addition of expansion teams?

A. The league divided into two divisions, East and West.

Q. Ernie Banks played in his 2,254th game in September of 1969 and broke the club record. Who held the mark until then?

A. Cap Anson.

Q. What was Ron Santo's routine for a victory dance when the team won at Wrigley Field?

A. He jumped in the air and clicked his heels three times.

Q. What monumental historic event occurred on the same day the Cubs swept the Phillies in a double-header on July 20, 1969?

A. Neil Armstrong walked on the moon.

Q. Ernie Banks earned a career-high hit in September of 1969 at Wrigley Field. What was the number?

A. 2,500.

Q. How many consecutive games had Billy Williams played up to April 30, 1970?

A. He stepped on the field for 1,000 times in a row.

Q. Williams was second in the 1970 MVP race to which famous player?

A. Johnny Bench.

Q. The Pirates hosted the Cubs in the last game ever played at Forbes Field in Pittsburgh in 1970. What was unique about that day?

A. The Cubs were also the guests of the Pirates at the opening of Forbes in 1909.

Q. Billy Williams' streak of consecutive games played (1,117) was surpassed by only four players. Who are they?

A. Lou Gehrig, Everett Scott, Cal Ripken, Jr., and Steve Garvey.

Q. Who was the first Cubs player to sign a contract for $100,000 in a season?

A. Billy Williams.

Q. Ron Santo revealed in 1971 that he suffered from which disease?

A. Diabetes.

Q. Which Cubs pitcher tied the club record of six home runs by a player in that position?

A. Ferguson Jenkins.

Q. Jenkins holds the all-time Cubs record for career strikeouts. How many does he have?

A. 2,038.

Q. Which player is in second place on the strikeout list?

A. Charlie Root.

Q. Utility man Carmen Fanzone had musical talent to complement his abilities on the field. What was his specialty?

A. He was a professional trumpet player.

Q. Reverend Jesse Jackson accused the Cubs of racism for not hiring Ernie Banks as team manager. What was P. K. Wrigley's reply?

A. He stated that Banks was "too nice" to be a big-league manager.

Q. Bill Madlock won two batting titles while playing for the Cubs. How long did he wear a Chicago uniform?

A. Only three seasons, from 1974 to 1976.

Q. In what year did longtime Wrigley Field announcer Pat Pieper die?

A. 1974. He had been part of the Cubs since 1904, when he started with the club as a vendor at West Side Grounds. He was the voice of Cubs games since 1916.

Q. Who was the last pitcher to throw a perfect game against the Cubs?

A. Sandy Koufax in 1965.

Q. Which player held the record for single-season home runs and RBIs up to 1988?

A. Hack Wilson. Sammy Sosa broke both of Wilson's records.

Q. Which local paper is credited with dubbing the hometown team the "Cubs?"

A. The *Chicago Daily News*.

Q. How many home runs did Ryne Sandberg have in his 1984 MVP season?

A. 19.

Q. Who was manager when the Cubs won the Eastern Division title in 1989?

A. Don Zimmer.

Q. Who was the last Cub's player to win the Cy Young award?

A. Greg Maddux in 1992.

Q. Andy McPhail was general manager of what other team before taking the helm with the Cubs in 1994?

A. Minnesota Twins.

Q. Who were "the Daily Double" in the 1984 season, and who named them?

A. Bob Dernier and Ryne Sandberg, named by announcer Harry Caray.

Q. Who won the Cy Young award in 1984?

A. Rick Sutcliffe.

Q. What was Sutcliffe's nickname?

A. "Redbeard."

Q. Who played second base in 1989 and is one of the most successful Cubs in team history?

A. Ryne Sandberg.

Q. What was right fielder Andre Dawson's nickname?

A. "The Hawk."

Q. Who played shortstop in the 1989 season?

A. Jeff Blauser.

Ryne Sandberg

CHAPTER FOUR

Another New Century—
Feels Like a Good Time to Win

Maybe the title will come home to Chicago this time around. The first five seasons of the 2000s brought a .490 winning percentage to the Cubs, and a Central Division title in 2003 (and, oh, so close to the World Series, again). There have been more signs that the decades-long rebuilding process could pay off and less evidence of the team's habit of letting it slip away.

Go Cubs!

Q. One of the two batters Cubs pitcher Jon Lieber faced in the 2001 All-Star game was New York's Derek Jeter. What was the result of that duel?

A. Jeter clobbered a home run.

Q. Who was manager of the Cubs in the 2001 season?

A. Don Baylor.

Q. Which players were first and second in batting average for the Cubs in 2001?

A. Sammy Sosa and Rondell White.

Q. Who was the starting pitcher on Opening Day in 2003?

A. Kerry Wood.

Q. The Cubs welcomed a new manager in the 2003 season. Who was he?

A. Dusty Baker.

Q. Where did Sammy Sosa hit his 500th home run?

A. Great American Ballpark in Cincinnati.

Q. How many home runs did Sosa hit in 2003?

A. Forty.

Q. Which team did the Cubs beat to win the 2003 National League pennant?

A. Pittsburgh Pirates.

Q. Which famous Cubs' number was retired after the 2003 season?

A. Ron Santo's.

Q. What is Wrigley Field's nickname?

A. "The Friendly Confines."

Q. What uniform number did Ron Santo wear?

A. 10.

Q. How many Cubs have had their numbers retired?

A. Four—Ernie Banks, Billy Williams, Ron Santo, and Ryne Sandberg.

Q. What is the distance to center field from home plate at Wrigley Field?

A. 400 feet.

Q. Since 1960, who holds the single-season record for saves?

A. Randy Myers.

Q. Which Cub's player has the most career home runs?

A. Sammy Sosa.

Q. In what year was Ryne Sandberg elected into the Hall of Fame?

A. 2005.

Q. How many Gold Glove awards did Sandberg win?

A. Nine.

Q. Which Cub's player tied Pete Rose for most hits in the National League in 1970?

A. Billy Williams and Rose both had 205 hits.

Q. Which player was league leader in stolen bases in 1939?

A. Stan Hack.

Q. Which Cubs pitcher had the most wins in the 1992 season?

A. Greg Maddux.

Q. Who was a Hall of Fame player and a manager for the Cubs?

A. Frank Chance.

Q. Which Cub's player was Rookie of the Year in 1989?

A. Outfielder Jerome Walton.

Q. Which Cubs player was nicknamed "the Penguin?"

A. Third baseman Ron Cey.

Q. Which team did Cey play for prior to the Cubs?

A. The Los Angeles Dodgers.

Q. Which Cub's player appeared in ten consecutive All-Star games?

A. Ryne Sandberg.

Q. Dave Kingman blasted one of the most memorable home runs ever at Wrigley Field on April 14, 1976. How far did the ball travel?

A. An estimated 530 feet.

Q. Only two Cubs have hit 500 or more home runs in their careers. Who are they?

A. Ernie Banks and Sammy Sosa.

Q. The Cubs started the 1997 season with a 0-14 record. Which team did they beat to score their first win?

A. The Mets.

Q. The Cubs were third in earned run average in 2004. When was the last time the team finished that high or better?

A. 1963, with a second-place mark.

Q. How many homers did the Cubs hit in the 2004 season?

A. 235.

Q. Why was Sammy Sosa ejected from a game against the Tampa Bay Devil Rays in June of 2003?

A. The umpires found cork in his bat.

Q. What is the name of the pitcher selected by the Cubs in the first round of the 1999 amateur draft?

A. Ben Christiansen of Wichita State.

Q. Sammy Sosa was the third youngest player in history to hit 500 home runs, when he did it at age 34 and 143 days. Which players reached the mark at younger ages?

A. Jimmie Foxx (32 years) and Willie Mays (34 years and 130 days).

MORE GREAT TITLES FROM TRAILS BOOKS

SPORTS

After They Were Packers, Jerry Poling

Always a Badger: The Pat Richter Story, Vince Sweeney

Baseball in Beertown: America's Pastime in Milwaukee, Todd Mishler

Badger Sports Trivia Teasers, Jerry Minnich

Before They Were the Packers: Green Bay's Town Team Days, Denis J. Gullickson and Carl Hanson

Chicago Bears Trivia Teasers, Steve Johnson

Cold Wars: 40+Years of Packer-Viking Rivalry, Todd Mishler

Green Bay Packers Titletown Trivia Teasers, Don Davenport

Mean on Sunday: The Autobiography of Ray Nitschke, Robert W. Wells

Mudbaths and Bloodbaths: The Inside Story of the Bears-Packers Rivalry, Gary D 'Amato & Cliff Christl

Packers By the Numbers: Jersey Numbers and the Players Who Wore Them, John Maxymuk

Vagabond Halfback: The Life and Times of Johnny Blood McNally, Denis J. Gullickson

ACTIVITY GUIDES

Biking Illinois: 60 Great Road and Trail Rides, David Johnsen

Biking Iowa: 50 Great Road and Trail Rides, Bob Morgan

Biking Wisconsin: 50 Great Road and Trail Rides, Steve Johnson

Great Iowa Walks: 50 Strolls, Rambles, Hikes and Treks, Lynn L. Walters

Great Minnesota Walks: 49 Strolls, Rambles, Hikes, and Treks, Wm. Chad McGrath

Great Wisconsin Walks: 45 Strolls, Rambles, Hikes, and Treks, Wm. Chad McGrath

Paddling Illinois: 64 Great Trips by Canoe and Kayak, Mike Svob

Paddling Iowa: 96 Great Trips by Canoe and Kayak, Nate Hoogeveen

Paddling Northern Wisconsin: 82 Great Trips by Canoe and Kayak, Mike Svob

Paddling Southern Wisconsin: 83 Great Trips by Canoe and Kayak, Mike Svob

Walking Tours of Wisconsin's Historic Towns, Lucy Rhodes, Elizabeth McBride, Anita Matcha

Wisconsin's Outdoor Treasures: A Guide to 150 Natural Destinations, Tim Bewer

Wisconsin Underground, Doris Green

TRAVEL GUIDES

Classic Wisconsin Weekends, Michael Bie

Great Indiana Weekend Adventures, Sally McKinney

Great Iowa Weekend Adventures, Mike Whye

Great Midwest Country Escapes, Nina Gadomski

Great Minnesota Taverns, David K. Wright & Monica G. Wright

Great Minnesota Weekend Adventures, Beth Gauper

Great Weekend Adventures, the Editors of Wisconsin Trails

Great Wisconsin Taverns: 101 Distinctive Badger Bars, Dennis Borer

Tastes of Minnesota: A Food Lover's Tour, Donna Tabbert Long

The Great Indiana Touring Book: 20 Spectacular Auto Trips, Thomas Huhti
The Great Iowa Touring Book: 27 Spectacular Auto Trips, Mike Whye
The Great Minnesota Touring Book: 30 Spectacular Auto Trips, Thomas Huhti
The Great Wisconsin Touring Book: 30 Spectacular Auto Tours, Gary Knowles
Twin Cities Restaurant Guide, Carla Waldemar
Wisconsin Family Weekends: 20 Fun Trips for You and the Kids, Susan Lampert Smith
Wisconsin Lighthouses: A Photographic and Historical Guide, Ken and Barb Wardius
Wisconsin's Hometown Flavors, Terese Allen
Wisconsin Waterfalls, Patrick Lisi
Up North Wisconsin: A Region for All Seasons, Sharyn Alden

HOME & GARDEN

Creating a Perennial Garden in the Midwest, Joan Severa
Eating Well in Wisconsin, Jerry Minnich
Midwest Cottage Gardening, Frances Manos
Northwoods Cottage Cookbook, Jerry Minnich
Wisconsin Country Gourmet, Marge Snyder & Suzanne Breckenridge
Wisconsin Garden Guide, Jerry Minnich
Wisconsin Wildfoods: 100 Recipes for Badger State Bounties, John Motoviloff

GIFT BOOKS

Celebrating Door County's Wild Places, The Ridges Sanctuary
Madison, Photography by Brent Nicastro
Milwaukee, Photography by Todd Dacquisto
Spirit of the North: A Photographic Journey Through Northern Wisconsin, Richard Hamilton Smith
The Spirit of Door County: A Photographic Essay, Darryl R. Beers

LEGENDS & LORE

Driftless Spirits: Ghosts of Southwest Wisconsin, Dennis Boyer
Haunted Wisconsin, Michael Norman and Beth Scott
Hunting the American Werewolf, Linda S. Godfrey
The Beast of Bray Road: Tailing Wisconsin's Werewolf, Linda S. Godfrey
The Poison Widow: A True Story of Sin, Strychnine, & Murder, Linda S. Godfrey
The W-Files: True Reports of Wisconsin's Unexplained Phenomena, Jay Rath

For a free catalog, phone, write, or e-mail us.

Trails Books
A Division of Big Earth Publishing
923 Williamson Street, Madison, WI 53703
800.258.5830 • www.trailsbooks.com